Amazing Writers

Level 4
CEF B2

D1258489

Text by
Katerina Mestheneou

Series edited by
Fiona MacKenzie

Collins

HarperCollins Publishers
77–85 Fulham Palace Road
Hammersmith London W6 8JB

10 9 8 7 6 5 4 3 2 1

Original text
© The Amazing People Club Ltd

Adapted text
© HarperCollins Publishers Ltd 2014

ISBN: 978-0-00-754506-3

Find out more about HarperCollins and the environment at
www.harpercollins.co.uk/green

◆ CONTENTS ◆

♦ INTRODUCTION ♦

Collins Amazing People Readers are collections of short stories. Each book presents the life story of five or six people whose lives and achievements have made a difference to our world today. The stories are carefully graded to ensure that you, the reader, will both enjoy and benefit from your reading experience.

You can choose to enjoy the book from start to finish or to dip into your favourite story straight away. Each story is entirely independent.

After every story a short timeline brings together the most important events in each person's life into one short report. The timeline is a useful tool for revision purposes.

Words which are above the required reading level are underlined the first time they appear in each story. All underlined words are defined in the glossary at the back of the book. Levels 1 and 2 take their definitions from the *Collins COBUILD Essential English Dictionary* and levels 3 and 4 from the *Collins COBUILD Advanced English Dictionary.*

To support both teachers and learners, additional materials are available online at www.collinselt.com/readers.

The Amazing People Club®

Collins Amazing People Readers are adaptations of original texts published by The Amazing People Club. The Amazing People Club is an educational publishing house. It was founded in 2006 by educational psychologist and management leader Dr Charles Margerison and publishes books, eBooks, audio books, iBooks and video content, which bring readers 'face to face' with many of the world's most inspiring and influential characters from the fields of art, science, music, politics, medicine and business.

◆ The Grading Scheme ◆

The Collins COBUILD Grading Scheme has been created using the most up-to-date language usage information available today. Each level is guided by a brand new comprehensive grammar and vocabulary framework, ensuring that the series will perfectly match readers' abilities.

		CEF band	Pages	Word count	Headwords
Level 1	elementary	A2	64	5,000–8,000	approx. 700
Level 2	pre-intermediate	A2–B1	80	8,000–11,000	approx. 900
Level 3	intermediate	B1	96	11,000–15,000	approx. 1,100
Level 4	upper intermediate	B2	112	15,000–19,000	approx. 1,700

For more information on the Collins COBUILD Grading Scheme, including a full list of the grammar structures found at each level, go to www.collinselt.com/readers/gradingscheme.

Also available online: Make sure that you are reading at the right level by checking your level on our website (www.collinselt.com/readers/levelcheck).

Voltaire

• ◆ •

1694–1778

the French writer who believed in social and
religious freedom

All through my life, one thing was important to me and that was freedom. Freedom to belong to any religion, freedom to work and earn a living, and most importantly, freedom of speech. I always said and wrote exactly what I thought.

♦ ◆ ♦

I was born in Paris, France on 21ˢᵗ November 1694 and I was the youngest of five children. My parents named me François-Marie and although my family name was Arouet, later as a writer, I chose the name Voltaire and that is how I am still known. My father, François Arouet was a public <u>official</u>, a lawyer, and my mother, Marie Marguerite d'Aumart, who died when I was 7 years old, came from an <u>aristocratic</u> family. Even though my father was considered to be <u>upper-middle class</u> and not part of the <u>aristocracy</u>, we lived well and did not have any financial problems. When I was 10 years old, in

1704, I started going to school at the *Collège Louis-le-Grand*. Here I was educated by Catholic priests and I discovered that I loved literature, theatre and writing, especially writing poetry and plays. From an early age I knew I wanted to become a professional writer. My father had other ideas – for some reason he did not want his son to follow a literary career – and so I was not allowed to continue studying what I loved. Instead, my father wanted me to become a lawyer and in 1711, when I left school, he found me a job in Paris as an assistant to a notary – a type of lawyer.

However, instead of learning about the law, I spent my time secretly studying and writing poetry. When I wasn't writing, I spent my time with friends. I soon found out that I was able to write in a way that amused people and I wrote funny poems about well-known people – poems that often lacked respect and were sometimes even rude. When my father discovered what I was really doing, he was furious. He was angry, not only because I had lied to him but also because he did not approve of my friends. In 1713, he sent me away to Caen in Normandy to study law.

While I was in Normandy, my father arranged for me to move to the Netherlands to work as a secretary for the French Ambassador. In the Netherlands, I met a young French woman called Catherine Olympe Dunoyer who was a <u>Protestant</u> refugee. In France, the only religion that was allowed was <u>Catholicism</u>. If you were not Catholic, you could be punished. Catherine and her family had gone to live in the Netherlands, which was mainly Protestant, where they were safe. We loved each other and wanted to run away and get married. My father discovered our plans and stopped us. Once again he was angry with me. At the age of 19, in disgrace, I was sent back to France, where my father thought he could control me.

◆ ◆ ◆

My relationship with my father had never been very good and I felt increasingly bitter and angry with the way he kept interfering in my life. I could not support myself because I had no money of my own and so I was forced to do what he wanted. I was also unhappy with the way French society was organized. For the past 50 years, France had been ruled by King Louis XIV. He believed that his right to be king had

King Louis XIV of France

come from God. He also believed that God only supported Catholics and that every other religion should be forbidden. This made me furious because I completely refused to accept that God was only in favour of one religion. To me, it was impossible. I believed in a different kind of society – one where everybody had the same rights, no matter what their religion, gender or social class was. Only the aristocracy and the Church had rights in France and, thinking it was most unfair, I expressed my feelings in the things I wrote. In a country where there was no social freedom, this was dangerous and probably not very wise.

My writing became more <u>satirical</u> as I criticized the church, and the king and his <u>advisors</u>, and I started to make enemies. My father decided to send me away again and I went to stay with the Marquis de Saint-Ange, a friend who lived in the country. I stayed there for some months and when I came back in 1715, my father tried to introduce me to a new circle of friends that he thought would have a better influence on me. I joined the <u>elite</u> social circle – the Court Sceaux – of a woman called the Duchesse du Maine. Here I found that many people admired my satirical humour, which naturally encouraged me to write more, and I started to become famous. The following year, in 1716, I made fun of the Duc d'Orléans, who was ruling the country until the king was old enough to do it himself. Louis XIV had died and King Louis XV was only five years old. The Duke was so annoyed by what I had written that he <u>exiled</u> me to a place called Tulle, which was about 480 kilometres from Paris. After a short while, he let me come back home.

Then, in 1717, I was arrested for having written an offensive poem about members of the ruling aristocracy. I was sent to the Bastille, which was a prison in the middle of Paris, for 11 months. Conditions there were terrible. It was full of mad people and rats carrying all kinds of disease. Being locked up didn't stop me from wanting to write about everything that I thought was wrong with French life. While I was in prison, I wrote my first play, called *Oedipe*, and I started to write *La Henriade*, which was a long poem that I didn't publish until 1723. When I came out of the Bastille in 1718, *Oedipe* was performed for the first time and it was a great success. It was about this time that I adopted the name Voltaire.

◆ ◆ ◆

In 1722, my father died and I started working for a man called Cardinal Guillaume Dubois as a secret diplomat. I hadn't stopped writing and managed to publish my poem, *La Henriade*. In 1726, I had an argument with a man called Chevalier de Rohan, who was from one of the most powerful aristocratic families in France. He said that I had insulted him and he had me arrested. I was sent to the Bastille once more. After a few weeks, I was given a choice. I could stay in prison or I could leave the country. I did not hesitate for a moment and decided to leave France and go to live in exile in England.

In England I soon learned the language and I started studying the work of John Locke, a British philosopher who I admired very much and whose ideas were very close to mine. He believed in social equality and he shared my belief that no king had a God-given right to rule. He was in favour of religious <u>tolerance</u> and thought that the church should not be part of a country's government. I also became fascinated by the work of Sir Isaac Newton, an English <u>physicist</u>, mathematician and, in his later years, philosopher. Through my writing, and all through my life, I tried to make the ideas of both of these great men better known. As a writer of plays, I was also interested in British theatre and in one writer in particular. His name was William Shakespeare. His plays were well known in Britain, but we had not heard of him in France. I loved the depth of his characters and the complicated plots, although I found the actual performances rather rough and lacking in style.

♦ ◆ ♦

In 1729, I returned to Paris and spent my time writing. I was writing serious articles now, not just the satirical poems of my youth, but texts about the lack of social and religious freedom in France, which I found shocking. Poor people were being exploited by those who were rich and I wrote that the king and the Church were responsible for this situation.

In 1732, I published a play called *Zaïre* which was a success, not only in France but also throughout Europe and I became very well known. The following year I published a collection of essays called *Letters On The English Nation* that I had been working on since my time in England. The articles were based on what I had seen during my exile. I wrote about how easy it was for educated men who were not from the aristocracy to follow various professions, about the freedom the press had to say whatever they wanted, and about the respect that was given to ordinary people. I suggested that it would be beneficial if other societies adopted these approaches to governing a country. My work, quite rightly, was viewed as a direct criticism of France and I found myself in trouble once again. To avoid being sent to the Bastille, I exiled myself from Paris and went to live far away in Lorraine in the north-east of France near Germany, Belgium and Luxembourg.

In the meantime, I had met a woman called Émilie du Châtelet. When we were introduced, she told me that she had read my books and we soon became close friends. She brought light and happiness to my life and I recognized in her a rare combination of <u>logic</u> and a passion for life. She was extremely well educated and was interested in science and literature. We went everywhere together – to the opera, the theatre and were even guests of the king. In Lorraine, I stayed at the Château de Cirey which was owned by Émilie's family.

The Château de Cirey, in Lorraine

◆ ◆ ◆

In 1735, I was given permission to return to Paris but I rather liked living in Lorraine and I decided to stay there. I had made a lot of money from some clever investments in banking and being rich gave me the opportunity to spend my time exactly as I wanted. Because of Émilie's interest in literature and science, we collected over 21,000 books. She worked hard on translating many scientific books from English to French and also read many books on philosophy and mathematics. We spent much time discussing philosophical and scientific theories, sometimes disagreeing. In 1738, with Émilie's help, I published a book called *Elements of the Philosophy of Newton* which helped to make his theories of gravity known to people outside the world of science.

◆ ◆ ◆

In 1742, I was sent by King Louis XV to Prussia on a secret trip to encourage the new king – Frederick II – to fight on the side of France in the War of the Austrian Succession. This was a series of wars lasting from 1740 until 1748 that began with the death of Charles VI, who was the Holy Roman Emperor. The wars were to decide who should take his place, as many royal figures thought they had the right to do so. Before Frederick had become king, he had read and enjoyed some of my work. He started writing to me and we became friends. I was successful in persuading him to fight on the side of France, and King Louis XV, who had never liked me personally, decided he would give me his attention once more. I was welcomed back into the elite social circles in France. From science, I turned my interest to history and, in 1745, King Louis XV made me the <u>Royal Historiographer</u> of France. A year later, I was elected to the French Academy. This institution had been set up in 1634 by Cardinal de Richelieu, who was the chief advisor of King Louis XIII, to protect the quality of literature and language.

In 1750, I was feeling unwelcome in Paris and disappointed with my life. Émilie had died the year before and I was terribly upset. Some of my recent plays had not been popular and although I was generally accepted in the royal court, there were very many people there who did not like me and certainly did not trust me. I had always found it difficult to keep my opinions to myself and I was constantly in trouble for having said or written <u>tactless</u> or cruel things about famous aristocrats or members of the Church. When my friend Frederick II invited me to go to his court in Potsdam near Berlin to be his <u>official</u> poet and philosopher, I accepted.

In the beginning things went well for me there. I wrote *The Age of Louis XIV* in 1751 and then the following year a short story called *Micromegas* was published. But then I began to quarrel with a man called Maupertuis who was President of the Scientific Academy in Berlin. I thought he was ridiculous and stupid and I wrote a long article about him which, although funny, was also really quite offensive. Frederick was furious with me and forbade me from ever coming to Berlin again. I left Prussia on 26th March 1753 and by the time I was nearing Paris, news of Frederick's anger had reached King Louis XV. He did not allow me to enter the city of Paris so I had to make other plans.

♦ ◆ ♦

In 1754, I went to Geneva in Switzerland where I bought a large estate called Les Délices and I continued writing and producing plays. I met Jean-Jacques Rousseau who was a political philosopher and a composer, whose ideas later had great influence. However, Rousseau and I started to have serious philosophical disagreements. A recommendation by him that theatre was completely unnecessary and even harmful was partly responsible for theatrical performances being banned in Geneva and, without the theatre, I felt there was no reason for me to stay. In addition, in my usual satirical way, I had made the Swiss feel uneasy. By 1758, it was time for me to leave.

I moved back to France to a village called Ferney, which was close to the border with Switzerland. I bought a large house and land where I entertained many important, influential people who came to watch my plays. I also supported local industry so that the ordinary people of Ferney, who had no civil rights, could work and make a living. I wanted to help the local community in any way I could. Naturally, I experienced opposition from the local aristocracy, who thought I was causing trouble by behaving like a revolutionary. Later on, after the French Revolution, the ordinary people of Ferney changed the name of the village to Ferney-Voltaire and a statue of me with the words 'Patriarch of Ferney' was built.

I stayed in Ferney for 20 years and because of the work I wrote and published during this time people began to see me differently. In 1759, I published a short story called *Candide*, which became my most famous book. As well as writing professionally, I enjoyed writing letters and I wrote to a great many people. One of them was Catherine II – Catherine the Great – of Russia. I also started writing again to my old friend, Frederick II, who had, by this time, forgiven me. In addition to *Candide*, I also published many other books including the popular philosophical work *Dictionnaire Philosophique*, in 1764. This was followed by *L'Ingénu* in 1767 and *Questions sur l'Encyclopédie* which was published in nine books between 1770 and 1772.

When I was 83 years old, I decided to return to Paris. The year was 1778. My latest play, a tragedy called *Irène* was going to be performed and I wanted to be present for the rehearsals and preparation. On the day after I arrived in Paris, more than 300 people came to my house to visit me. Three months later, on 30th May, I died peacefully in my sleep. It appears that after being away for 28 years I had come back as a popular man – some people even called me a hero.

The Life of Voltaire

1694   Voltaire was born in Paris, France and given the name François-Marie Arouet. He was the youngest of five children, but sadly only three of his brothers and sisters survived.

1701   His mother, Marie, died.

1704–1711   At the age of 10, Voltaire was enrolled at the *Collège Louis-le-Grand*, where he was educated by Catholic priests. He expressed a love of literature and theatre, and a talent for writing poetry.

1711–1712   He wanted to study literature. However, his father had plans for him to study law. He agreed to study law, but, in the meantime, he wrote poetry in secret.

1713   His father sent him to Caen, Normandy when he discovered he had been writing poetry instead of studying law. Work was also arranged for Voltaire in the Netherlands as a secretary to the French ambassador. It was there that he planned to run away and marry Catherine Olympe Dunoyer, a French Protestant refugee. His father discovered their plans and sent him back to France.

1714   His satirical work started causing problems. His father sent him away again to live with the Marquis de Saint-Ange, who lived in the country.

1715   He returned to Paris and became involved with the famous 'Court of Sceaux', a social circle run by the Duchesse du Maine.

1716   He insulted the Duc d'Orléans and was exiled to Tulle.

1717   He was sent to the Bastille prison for writing an offensive poem about an aristocrat. He stayed there for 11 months and wrote his first play, *Oedipe*, and began to write *La Henriade*.

1718   He was released from the Bastille. Around that time, he chose the pen name Voltaire. *Oedipe* was first performed and was very successful.

1722–1723   His father died. Voltaire began working as a secret diplomat for Cardinal Guillaume Dubois. He travelled to Cambrai, Brussels and The Hague. He published his poem *La Henriade*.

1725   Voltaire was a guest at the wedding of King Louis XV.

1726–1728	He quarrelled with the aristocrat Chevalier de Rohan and was sent to prison at the Bastille. He was exiled to England. In England, Voltaire was recognized as a great writer.
1729	Voltaire returned to Paris.
1732	He published a play called *Zaïre*.
1733	Voltaire published a collection of essays called *Letters on the English Nation*. He went to Lorraine to avoid being sent to prison. He went to stay at the Château de Cirey, owned by his friend Émilie du Châtelet.
1735	He was given permission to return to Paris but he chose to stay at Cirey and only returned to Paris occasionally.
1738	*Elements of the Philosophy of Newton* was published.
1740–1743	Voltaire lived in Prussia and Brussels, where he worked as a diplomat.
1745	King Louis XV made him Royal Historiographer of France.
1746	He was elected to the French Academy.
1748	He published the philosophical tale *Zadig*.

1749   Émilie du Châtelet died.

1751   Voltaire moved to Potsdam in Germany. He became a philosopher and poet to his close friend, Frederick the Great. He published *The Age of Louis XIV.*

1752   He published *Micromegas.*

1753   A conflict began between Voltaire and Maupertuis. Voltaire was forced by Frederick II to leave Berlin and he slowly travelled to Paris.

1754   Louis XV refused to allow Voltaire into the city of Paris. Voltaire moved on to Geneva in Switzerland and bought a large estate named Les Délices. He met the philosopher Jean-Jacques Rousseau.

1758   He moved to Ferney in France after the local law in Geneva forbade theatre performances. He bought another estate and entertained many important guests at his home.

1759   He published his short story *Candide (ou l'Optimisme).*

1762   Voltaire began writing letters to Catherine II of Russia.

1763	He published *Treatise on Tolerance*.
1764	He published one of his most popular philosophical works, *Dictionnaire Philosophique*.
1767	The philosophical tale *L'Ingénu* was published.
1769	A new edition of the *Philosophical Dictionary* was published under the name *The Alphabet of Reason*.
1770–1772	*Questions sur l'Encyclopédie* was published in nine books.
1778	Voltaire returned to Paris. He lived to see the performance of his last play, a tragedy called *Irène*. He died three months later, aged 83.

Charlotte Brontë

◆ ◆ ◆

1816–1855

the woman who wrote *Jane Eyre*

Writing stories was a way to escape from the ugly, sad, miserable moments in life. Even though much of my work was based on my life experiences and included those difficult parts of it, my novels were also based on my dreams of love and happiness.

◆ ◆ ◆

I was born on 21ˢᵗ April 1816 in the village of Thornton, in West Yorkshire, England. I had four sisters – two were older than me and two were younger and I had a brother who was born a year after I was. My father, Patrick, was an <u>Anglican</u> <u>vicar</u> and my mother, Maria Branwell, was kept busy looking after her family. When I was 4 years old, we moved to a village not far away called Haworth, where my father had been given the position of <u>curate</u> at the village church. My mother had been unwell for some time and a year later, she died. We were looked after by her sister, who we called Aunt Branwell but whose name was Elizabeth.

My father, who was still very upset by my mother's death, had difficulty coping with us all. In 1824, he sent me and three of my sisters – Maria, Elizabeth and Emily – to a school, the Clergy Daughters School, that was for daughters of Anglican church employees. Maria, who was 10 years old, and Elizabeth, at the age of 9, went there first in July. Then, in September, my father sent me and Emily. I was 8 and Emily was only 6 years old. My other sister, Anne, and my brother, Branwell, stayed at home.

◆ ◆ ◆

The school was in a village called Cowan Bridge in the neighbouring county of Lancashire. None of the girls' parents had to pay for their daughters to go to this school – all the expenses were paid by the church – and for this reason, we were called <u>Charity</u> Children by the teachers and the other people who worked there. It was horrible and made us feel ashamed and stupid. We were all given a special ugly uniform to wear and every time we left the school, to go to church for example, it showed that we were Church Charity Children.

Life at the school was unpleasant and difficult. When we arrived, winter was approaching and as it got colder and colder, we suffered. We slept all together in one large room where there was no heating. In the morning when we got up, we had to wash in cold water – on the really cold mornings, and there were many of them, we had to break the ice that had formed overnight in the bowls of water. Our uniforms were not adequate for the cold weather and the damp that was everywhere reached through to our bones and froze us. On Sundays after we got up, we had to say <u>prayers</u> for an hour and a half. Then we had to go to church. The church was five kilometres away and we had to walk there and back in all weathers. Our thin clothes gave us no protection against the cold, wind, rain and snow. We were always cold and we never stopped being hungry, as we were never given enough food. The food that they did give us was of poor quality and it often made us sick.

Most of the teachers treated us badly. They seemed to enjoy punishing us for the slightest thing we did wrong. Many of the other girls were unkind, too. Emily and I were some of the youngest girls there and the older students often teased us and were cruel. We were all very unhappy.

Because of the bad conditions we were forced to live in at school, my sisters Maria and Elizabeth became ill with a terrible disease called tuberculosis, which affects the lungs. They were sent home to recover. Sadly, in June 1825, they both died. Emily and I stayed at school but in the autumn of the same year, when we also showed signs of having tuberculosis, we too were sent home. Luckily, we recovered.

◆ ◆ ◆

I was now the oldest child and I became responsible for looking after my brother and sisters. Without an adult looking after us – my father was busy with his job in the church – we spent our time in the countryside near our home doing whatever we wanted. We had all experienced a great deal of sadness with the deaths of our mother and then our two sisters and I began to dream of a better life. One day in 1826, my father gave my brother a set of wooden soldiers which we all enjoyed playing with. We invented an <u>imaginary</u> world that we called Angria and we made up detailed and very complicated stories about life there. We were perfectly aware of what real life consisted of, but our imaginations took us away from the long cold nights of the Yorkshire winter and the endless summers days when there was not much to occupy us. I soon started writing down the stories.

In 1831, when I was 14, my father decided that I should continue my education and he sent me away to school again. This time it was an enjoyable experience. Like the other teachers at Roe Head School, the <u>principal</u>, Miss Wooler, was a kind woman. Unlike my previous experience, I made friends, particularly with two girls, Ellen Nussey and Mary Taylor, who I stayed friends with for my entire life. While I was there, I wrote a short story called *The Green <u>Dwarf</u>*. I stayed at Roe Head for a year and then went back home to teach my sisters and brother.

♦ ♦ ♦

In 1835, aged 19, I had to earn some money and I went back to Roe Head School as an assistant teacher. Emily became a student there and then, when she came home after a year, Anne took her place. In 1837, Anne became ill and we both returned home. I started writing more seriously. In 1839, I met Edward, the brother of my friend Ellen Nussey, who was a vicar like my father. To my surprise he asked me to marry him, but I knew that if I became a vicar's wife, I would not be able to spend my time writing. I would have to spend all my time helping with the church and visiting the sick and the poor, so I refused his proposal. Shortly after that, another man also asked me to be his wife. I admit that it was nice to be asked but I wanted to see a wider world beyond the village and the Yorkshire countryside and I said no to him, too. I decided instead to become a <u>governess</u> to the children of rich families.

In 1839, my first job as governess was for a family called Sidgewick who lived in the town of Skipton. The child I was in charge of was a naughty little boy and I only stayed there for three months. After that, I went to a family in the city of Leeds, but I realized that being a governess was not the job I wanted to continue doing. I returned back home in 1841. One day I had an idea. I wanted to have a school of my own where my sisters would also be able to work. Our father thought it was a good idea but we needed more knowledge and experience before we could begin.

In 1843, Emily and I decided to go to a school in Brussels in Belgium called the Héger <u>Boarding School</u> run by Constantin Héger and his wife. Aunt Branwell helped to pay for our travel expenses and accommodation. We started studying French, German and music and, to help pay our fees, I taught English to the other students. It wasn't enough, though, and we started to get into debt. Later that year, a letter came from home with bad news. Aunt Branwell had died. Feeling very upset, we left Brussels and returned home. When our aunt's <u>will</u> was read, we discovered that she had left us some money. It was more than enough to pay off our debts and helped us feel a little bit less sad.

Then a letter arrived that made me truly happy. Mr Héger invited me to come back to his school to continue teaching. In the beginning I was excited and everything went well for me. I was made to feel welcome and I worked hard for a year, but gradually I started missing my home. At weekends, I went for long walks and many ideas came to me. I kept notes with the intention of writing a longer story but I felt unhappy in Brussels and in 1844, I decided to come home.

◆ ◆ ◆

For my father, life had become more difficult. He had lost most of his sight and he went to the city of Manchester for treatment. We still had some of the money that Aunt Branwell had left us in her will and my sisters and I decided to open the school we had been planning. Our house was large and we used a part of it for the school. Unfortunately, not even one pupil enrolled, which was a huge disappointment and we had to abandon our plan.

In 1846, Emily, Anne and I published a collection of our poetry, paying the publishing costs ourselves. There were very few women authors and it was not really socially acceptable for women to publish books. In addition, there were many people who thought that women were not capable of producing work of any quality. To avoid both of these problems, we used the names Currer, Ellis and Acton Bell to hide our gender. We used our real initials, so I was Currer Bell, Emily was Ellis Bell and Anne was Acton Bell. Although only a few copies sold, it was encouraging and we continued to write. In 1847, I completed my first novel, called *The Professor*, which I had started when I came back from Brussels. I sent it to a publisher, who rejected it, and

it wasn't published until after my death. The publishers did say, however, that they would be interested to see a longer book from 'Currer Bell'.

I had been working on a full-length story called *Jane Eyre*. It was about a young woman who had been badly treated at boarding school and then became a governess. She developed strong feelings for her employer, who she later married. I sent the story to the publishers in August 1847. They accepted it, and six weeks later it was published. Within a short time, I heard that positive reviews had been written about *Jane Eyre* and people were actually buying it. From the time when it was first read, there were questions about whether it had been written by a man or a woman. As people began to suspect that the author was female, the book was criticized for being coarse – meaning that it was rude and offensive, and not the 'kind of story' that should be written by a woman. I think that the publicity this caused actually helped the sales of the book. People wanted to see for themselves what was in the book that made it so unsuitable.

Meanwhile, my sisters too were having personal success as authors. In the same year, Emily wrote a book called *Wuthering Heights*, which was a vivid love story about jealous people looking for revenge. It was very successful. My other sister, Anne, wrote a book called *Agnes Grey* which was about the unfair treatment of women and animals. Again, as there had been with *Jane Eyre*, there was a great deal of discussion about whether these two books had been written by men or women. Because we had hidden our real identities, we were unable to celebrate our success in public but we enjoyed sharing our secret and we celebrated in private. However, Anne and I did visit our publishers in London and reveal who we were.

Sadly, my brother was not in any state to celebrate. He became severely ill with bronchitis – a chest infection that makes you cough. He also had tuberculosis – the disease that my two other sisters had died from – and in 1848, Branwell died. Within a short time, my sister Emily also got tuberculosis and she, too, died. Anne, my father and I were truly shocked and were suffering from the most terrible grief. To focus on something more positive, I finished a book called *Shirley* that I had started earlier. More pain followed, though, when a year later, Anne also died of tuberculosis. <u>Darkness</u> covered our home for the third time in two years. I was afraid and lonely too, having lost my best friends. My brother and five sisters had all died and I was scared that I would be the next one. When Emily died and then Anne, I stopped writing because my grief made it impossible for me to concentrate on anything.

Shirley was published in 1849. The following year, I went to London and met a writer called Elizabeth Gaskell, who introduced me to all the important people in London and became a good friend. In 1853, I wrote my third book, called *Villette*. The story was an emotional one about a young woman, a teacher, who travels abroad to work and falls in love with a man she cannot marry. Once again many people described the book as being coarse, as they were disturbed by the emotions I described, which they thought were unsuitable for a woman to write about. In general, though, *Villette* was recognized as being a serious book of good quality.

Several years before, a young man called Arthur Bell Nicholls had become a curate at my father's church, in Haworth. We had known each other for a long time and I didn't really think about him very much until one day in 1853, he asked me to marry him. My father didn't want me to marry him, partly because he was so poor – curates do not earn a lot of money. I refused his proposal. My friend in London, Elizabeth Gaskell, advised me to think again about my decision. She told me to use my head and not my heart. She believed in marriage, and she used her social influence to have Arthur's salary increased. I did think again and Arthur himself was determined to marry me. When he asked me again in January 1854, I accepted. My father changed his mind too, and six months later, in June 1854, we got married.

Within a few months, I was expecting a baby and I felt happy, as if my dreams were finally coming true. However, my good luck did not last, as I soon became ill. I started to feel tired, even in the middle of the day and then I started coughing. I developed a fever that made me think and say strange things. Arthur called the doctor, but he didn't have anything that would help me. As my pregnancy progressed, I became weaker and more ill. I knew I was going to die before my baby was born and this indeed happened on 31st March 1855. Before I died, I had time to look back on my life, which had been full of sickness, death and sadness. There had also been periods of happiness and great creativity. I spent a long time thinking of my books and those of my sisters and I wondered if anyone would remember us and if our books would still be popular in later years. I truly hoped they would be.

The Life of Charlotte Brontë

1816   Charlotte was born in Thornton, West Yorkshire, England. She was the third of six children; there were five sisters and one brother.

1820   The family moved to Haworth, as her father became curate of St Michael and All Angels Church.

1821   Charlotte's mother died when Charlotte was 5. The Brontë children were left in the care of her mother's sister, Elizabeth.

1824   Charlotte, Emily, Maria and Elizabeth all attended the Clergy Daughters' School at Cowan Bridge in Lancashire. However, the conditions at the school were awful and the sisters' health began to decline.

1825   Sadly, both Maria and Elizabeth died of tuberculosis. Charlotte and Emily returned home.

1826   Charlotte's father bought a box of wooden soldiers for his son, Branwell. The four surviving children began playing with them and writing stories about an imaginary world called Angria.

1831 Charlotte enrolled at Roe Head School. She enjoyed her time there and made two lifelong friends. The following year, she returned home to teach her sisters.

1835 Charlotte became a junior teacher at Roe Head School to help support her family. Emily became a student at the school. Later that year, Emily returned home and Anne took her place at the school.

1837 Her sister, Anne, became ill and both sisters returned home.

1839 Charlotte turned down two proposals of marriage. She accepted a position as governess with a family called Sidgewick, but left after three months.

1841 She became a governess for the White family, and returned home after nine months.

1842 Charlotte and Emily travelled to Brussels and enrolled at a boarding school run by Constantin Héger and his wife. The sisters studied languages and music. In the same year, their aunt Elizabeth died and the sisters returned home.

1843 Charlotte returned alone to Héger's school. During that time, she started to miss her home.

1844   She returned home and started a school at
        the family's house in Haworth. However,
        no students enrolled.

1846   The three sisters published a collection
        of their poetry under the false names of
        Currer, Ellis and Acton Bell, to hide their
        gender. Only a few copies were sold.
        However, the sisters continued to write.

1847   Charlotte completed her first novel called
        The Professor. However, it was rejected
        by the publisher. She sent the publisher
        a second book, *Jane Eyre*, which was
        published. It became an immediate success.
        Emily's book, *Wuthering Heights*, and Anne's
        book, *Agnes Grey*, were also published.

1848   Charlotte and Anne visited their
        publishers in London and revealed their
        true identities. Around the same time,
        tragedy struck the Brontë household.
        Their brother, Branwell, and sister, Emily,
        died in the same year. Dealing with
        her grief, Charlotte began working on
        another novel, *Shirley*.

1849   Sadly, her sister Anne died. Charlotte's
        novel *Shirley* was published.

1850   She met the author Elizabeth Gaskell,
        who introduced Charlotte to London
        society. Elizabeth also wrote Charlotte's
        biography after her death.

1853   Charlotte's third novel, *Villette*, was
        published.

1854   Charlotte accepted the proposal of
        marriage from her father's curate, Arthur
        Bell Nicholls. They married in the same
        year, and she became pregnant with their
        first child.

1855   During her pregnancy, Charlotte's health
        began to decline. She died aged 38, along
        with her unborn child.

Mark Twain

◆ ◆ ◆

1835–1910

the man who wrote *Huckleberry Finn* and
Tom Sawyer

**My life was an interesting one. I worked at several jobs –
some of which I liked and some of which I was not very
good at. One thing stayed the same no matter what I did
or where I was, and that was my love of books.**

◆ ◆ ◆

I was born on 30ᵗʰ November 1835, in a tiny village called
Florida in Missouri, in the USA. My parents were John
and Jane Clemens and they named me Samuel Langhorne
Clemens. I later changed my name to Mark Twain and
that is how I am still known today. My father was a judge
but although we weren't poor, there wasn't any money to
buy things like books or toys. Life was sometimes difficult.
Medical advice and facilities were basic and there was little
protection against disease. I was the sixth of seven children
but several of my brothers and sisters died when they were
just babies or small children. Pleasant died when he was

6 months old, six years before I was born. When I was 3, my sister Margaret died and then Benjamin died in 1842, when I was 7. Each time I saw my parents upset at the death of another child it upset me and I realized at a very young age that, as well as being cruel, life could be short.

In 1839, when I was 4 years old, we moved to a place near the Mississippi River called Hannibal. It was a small community in the fast-developing area of the <u>Midwest</u>, between St Louis and Kansas City. It was an interesting place to grow up. Being on the Mississippi River, there was a lot of activity as <u>steamboats</u> came into the port three times a day. There was also a lot of violence and I witnessed death in the streets more than once. Just before my 12th birthday, in 1847, my father died from a disease called pneumonia. Suddenly we had no source of income. We didn't have enough money to buy food and clothes and so naturally there was no money to pay the fees at the private school I had been going to. It was time for me to start working.

♦ ◆ ♦

I found a job as an <u>apprentice</u> printer at a newspaper called the *Hannibal Courier*. The pay wasn't much, but it did allow me to feed myself. I stayed there for two years and learnt the basics of printing. Then in 1851, when I was 15, I started working with my brother Orion, who owned the *Hannibal Messenger*, a small newspaper that focused on local news stories and gossip. My work mainly involved printing, but occasionally I was allowed to write an article or help edit the work of other writers. It was at my brother's newspaper that I discovered I enjoyed writing.

As well as being a busy port, our town was also a <u>junction</u> for the new steam trains. After working on the *Messenger* for three years, I decided to travel and gain a wider experience of life. At the age of 18, I travelled to New York to see the USA's first World Fair. This was where the latest industrial and technological inventions from all over the world could be seen. It was a great event, showing what can be done by hard work. It made me realize there was a big world out there, but before I could tour it, I needed to earn some money.

I moved from New York to Philadelphia and I got a job as a printer. I also spent time in St Louis and Cincinnati, all the time working and gaining valuable experience. Moving from place to place kept me sharp, as I watched people and learnt about life. I spent my evenings at the local library, reading a far wider range of topics than was available in any school. As my formal education had been limited, teaching myself by reading and gaining life experience was the basis for my own writing. In 1855, I went to stay with my brother Orion who was now living in Iowa, and I continued printing and writing for the next two years.

♦ ◆ ♦

By 1857, I felt it was time to move on and gain more experience. I really wanted to explore more of the world and my intention was to go to Brazil. I got as far as New Orleans. I met a river boat captain called Horace Bixby, who taught me how to be a pilot on a river steamboat. It was difficult, skilled work but it was very well paid and in total I spent four years on the river. Life on the Mississippi was a rich source of stories and at each port, people shared

A steamboat on the Mississippi River

views and news. Sailing up and down the 2,000 miles of the river taught me a lot.

In 1859, I earned my steamboat pilot's licence. One day in the same year, I learned that my brother Henry had been killed. The steamboat he was on, the *Pennsylvania* had exploded. I felt particularly bad because it was I who had encouraged Henry to work on steamboats. His death was tragic, but steamboats were essential, as they were the basis of trade and economic development. On either side of the river were the <u>plantations</u> where African slaves worked in the fields growing cotton and <u>tobacco</u> under the hot sun. I had grown up in a state of the USA where it was normal practice to have slaves working on the plantations. As a child I had not really questioned whether <u>slavery</u> was right or not. Now for the first time, I began to form an opinion about it and as the <u>Civil War</u> came closer, I heard other people's views, too. I gathered a lot of information for a book I was writing called *Life on The Mississippi*.

In 1861, when the Civil War started, the boat I was working on was taken by the <u>Confederate Army</u>. In the beginning, I had some sympathy for their <u>cause</u> and joined them as a volunteer soldier but, after two weeks, I decided I was not a fighting man and I left. Trading on the river had stopped because of the war, which meant that I no longer had a job. In 1861, I joined my brother Orion, who was now in Nevada. He had a senior position in President Lincoln's government. Spending time with him, I came to realize the <u>injustice</u> of slavery and the need for change.

◆ ◆ ◆

In 1862, I moved on to Virginia City and got a job as a silver <u>miner</u>. I had dreams of becoming rich and being able to buy whatever I wanted. It was wild country and it was the source for my book, *Roughing It* which I wrote later on. I wasn't very good at being a miner and I had no money at all. When I was offered a job as a newspaper reporter on the *Territorial Enterprise*, I accepted it at once. It was there that I realized I needed a new name. Samuel Langhorne Clemens was not an easy name to remember or say and so, in 1863, I changed it to Mark Twain. I liked the sound of the name but it was actually used by riverboat men to describe the depth of water. Water was measured in fathoms – a fathom was 1.85 metres deep and 'mark twain' meant water that was 2 fathoms deep – 3.7 metres. Later I continued my journey west, and arriving in San Francisco in California, I found a job as a journalist. San Francisco was an amazing place on a beautiful bay, where the noise of construction could be heard everywhere as the city was being built. Here there were people of many nationalities who had settled. Farmers, men searching for gold and those trying to make their fortune by playing cards lived side-by-side. People worked hard during the day and then played hard in the evening.

Thanks to my writing skills, I worked for several local newspapers. The *San Francisco Morning Call* was one of them. Also, I wrote for *The Daily Morning* and *Alta California*. At last, I was earning enough money so that I could focus on writing and I went in search of great stories. Later, I also worked for *The Sacramento Union*. In the meantime, I wrote a number of short stories – one that became well-known was called *Jim Smiley and his Jumping Frog*, and it was published in the *New York Saturday Press* on 18th November 1865.

♦ ♦ ♦

The following year, I went to Hawaii on the ship the *Ajax* which was making its first voyage. Arriving at these islands in the Pacific Ocean, I found myself in the most perfect, beautiful place. The beaches, the sun and easy lifestyle there tempted me to stay but I had always had difficulty staying in one place. I constantly felt the need to explore new places and meet people and then write about my experiences. A Californian paper sent me to Panama. I was becoming well-known now as a writer and as my stories were becoming more popular, it seemed that people liked my <u>satirical</u> humour and style.

Then suddenly, in 1867, I was asked to tour the Mediterranean by boat and write about what I saw. This was an experience that was too good to refuse. I crossed the Atlantic in a ship called *Quaker City* and then spent five months observing and writing as I visited the countries of Europe and the Middle East. Combining work with tourism and pleasure gave me the most amazing opportunity to explore my creativity. I sent back regular reports to the American newspapers, and when I came back to the USA after my trip, I was surprised to find that I had become famous. I also realized that there was more than enough material from my trip for me to write a whole book, and this is what I did. My first book, *The Innocents Abroad*, was published in 1869 and became a bestseller.

In the same year as my visit to Europe, 1867, an event occurred which really changed my life – I met a special woman, Olivia Langdon, who was the daughter of a rich New Yorker. Her brother, who I had met on board the *Quaker City*, introduced us in New York and in February of 1870, we got married and went to live in Buffalo. On the day of my wedding, I received 4,000 dollars in <u>royalties</u> from my book. Olivia's father was also generous, giving me <u>shares</u> in a newspaper called the *Buffalo Express*. Towards the end of that year, our son, Langdon, was born.

With the income from my royalties and the *Buffalo Express*, I was able to write full time for a living. After all, I now had plenty of experience. *Roughing It* was published in 1872 and just when life was looking good, tragedy struck when Langdon, aged 19 months, died of the disease diphtheria. I was haunted by terrible thoughts. Were we in some way responsible for his death? Should we have done more to prevent the infection? I remembered how upset my mother and father were when my brothers and sisters had died and, just like my parents, I experienced many days of <u>darkness</u>. To cope with the sadness, I worked day and night. After our daughter, Susy was born in 1872, we decided to move house and get away from the memories. In 1873, we moved to a place called Hartford and built a house with 19 rooms. There, we were fortunate to have two more daughters, Clara and Jean.

With a strong home life, I was able to concentrate on writing and I was filled with ideas. Each day, I worked on a new idea for my stories. I published one of them in 1876. It was called *The Adventures of Tom Sawyer*, and it was very popular, with many copies being sold. I wrote more books: *Tramp Abroad* in 1880, which was based on a tour of Europe I had done in 1878, and *The Prince and the Pauper*, published in 1881.

In 1883, I started my own publishing company which was called Charles L. Webster & Co. In the same year, I published *The Adventures of Huckleberry Finn* and *Life on the Mississippi*. I kept writing and published *A Connecticut Yankee in King Arthur's Court* in 1889. This was a mixture of science fiction and history and received quite a lot of criticism and I started to experience financial problems. The publishing house I owned, managed by my nephew, ran into problems. Several bad business decisions had been made that led to losses. In addition, I had invested heavily in the Paige typesetter which was a machine with keys that prints letters onto paper. Unfortunately, new technology came along which replaced it and I lost all the money I had invested. I needed to start writing again.

I wrote *The American Claimant* with another writer called William Dean in 1891 and *Tom Sawyer Abroad by Huck Finn* in 1894 but still needed to earn more money. In 1894, I went on a worldwide tour including visits to Canada, Australia, India and South Africa. These proved to be interesting and challenging experiences, which gave me the inspiration to write again and I published my last novel, *Pudd'nhead Wilson* in 1894. However, because of continued financial difficulties I <u>filed for bankruptcy</u> in 1894. Two years later, my daughter Susy died of a disease called meningitis. My wife and I were filled with grief. I could not stay at home, so once more I went abroad and I wrote a book about travel called *Following the Equator*.

◆ ◆ ◆

As well as writing, I became interested in politics. I was unhappy about some of the <u>imperialist</u> activities the government was involved in, for example when they tried to gain control of the Philippines. Some of my writings against the government were controversial and there were editors who refused to publish my work. I was even called a <u>traitor</u> because some people thought I was against our national beliefs. Once again, travel saved me and in 1903, we decided to go to Italy for a holiday. While we were there, my wife became ill and got steadily worse. After 34 years of marriage, Olivia died in 1904. Dark days were made worse by business worries. Things looked black for me. I had no wife, no money and nothing to support me when I grew old. I decided to go on another trip and see some friends. I visited Berlin, Paris, Vienna and Florence. On the way I gave lectures and speeches and received awards. However, one can only travel so far and for so long. Eventually, we all need to return somewhere comfortable and I decided that the place I would call my last home was New York.

For me, New York was fascinating. They say that money does not grow on trees but it certainly seemed to grow near those in Wall Street – the area of the city where financial business was done. The noise and fuss of the city was an inspiration to me. I also liked the way you could look at a person and see from the expression on their face exactly what they were feeling. From my window and during my walks I watched. From here I wrote the story of my life.

In 1905, I was 70 years old. On the night of my birthday we had a party at an excellent restaurant called Delmonico's. President Teddy Roosevelt came to New York for the occasion and it was a special evening in a special city. Even though I had written about my life, I had more living to do. In 1907, I was given an <u>Honorary</u> <u>Doctor of Letters</u> degree from Oxford University in England, to add to the one I had been given six years before by Yale University, here in the USA. I found it funny, thinking about the fact that I had finished school when I was 12 years old. The following year, I moved to Redding in Connecticut and then in 1909, Jean, my youngest daughter died.

I always remembered a story my parents had told me when I was a young boy. On the day that I was born there was a bright light in the sky that wasn't normally there. My parents wondered what it meant. Could it be a special sign from above to celebrate my birth? Their neighbours and friends came around to our house and some of them had great fears that perhaps this was the end of the world. Everyone had an opinion but what was the reality? For some, it was a time of hope. For others, it was a time of fear but soon, the great light disappeared and people went back to work and their normal lives. Later we learnt that the bright light was Halley's Comet, which is visible from Earth every 74 or 75 years. I knew that it was due to make an appearance again soon and I thought that it signalled the time for me to go. I was right. Halley's Comet appeared again on 20th April 1910. The very next day I had a heart attack and died. I would have been most disappointed if my death had not happened as my birth had – with a bright unusual light appearing in the sky.

The Life of Mark Twain

1835   Mark Twain was born on 30th November in Florida, Missouri. His parents named him Samuel Langhorne Clemens. He later changed his name to Mark Twain.

1839   His family moved to Hannibal, which in 1839 became a town with its own local government offices. Images of Hannibal are reflected in the Tom Sawyer and Huckleberry Finn books.

1847   His father died before Mark's 12th birthday.

1851   Mark started working at the *Hannibal Messenger* newspaper as a printer.

1853   He travelled to St. Louis, New York and Philadelphia.

1857   He moved south and worked as an apprentice Mississippi River pilot for two years. He saw the cotton plantations and saw what slavery meant. He gathered information for his book called *Life on the Mississippi*.

1858   His younger brother, Henry, was killed in an explosion on the steamboat *Pennsylvania*.

1859   Mark received his steamboat licence and continued working on the Mississippi River for the next two years.

1861   He became involved in the American Civil War. He trained with the Confederate Army, as a volunteer soldier for two weeks.

1862   He travelled west through Nevada and worked briefly in mining before becoming a reporter at a Virginia City newspaper, the *Territorial Enterprise*.

1863   He changed his name to Mark Twain.

1864   Mark arrived in California and lived in San Francisco, where he worked as a journalist.

1865   He wrote a short story about *Jim Smiley and his Jumping Frog* and it was published in the *New York Saturday Press*.

1866   Employed by the newspaper *The Sacramento Union*, Mark sailed to Hawaii and wrote of his travel adventures.

1867   He crossed the Atlantic in a ship called *Quaker City* and spent five months writing for American newspapers about the countries of Europe and the Middle East. He met Olivia, his future wife. They became engaged the following year.

1869   His first book, *The Innocents Abroad*, was published and became a bestseller.

1870   He married Olivia Langdon and a son, Langdon, was born.

1872   His book, *Roughing It*, was published. His daughter, Susy, was born, but sadly his son died from diphtheria.

1873   The family moved to Hartford, Connecticut.

1874   Their daughter Clara was born.

1876   *The Adventures of Tom Sawyer* was published.

1878   Mark went on his second tour of Europe. The trip provided material for his book *A Tramp Abroad*.

1880   Their fourth child, a daughter, Jean was born. *A Tramp Abroad* was published.

1881   *The Prince and the Pauper* was published.

1883   *Life on the Mississippi* was published. A year later, he started his own publishing company Charles L. Webster & Co. Mark published the most famous of his works, *The Adventures of Huckleberry Finn*.

1885   Mark published the *Personal Memoirs of Ulysses S. Grant*, shortly after the death of President Grant.

1888   Mark earned his first Master of Art degree
        from Yale University.

1889   *A Connecticut Yankee in King Arthur's Court*
        was published and received criticism.

1894   His last novel, *Pudd'nhead Wilson*, was
        published. Due to financial difficulties,
        Mark filed for bankruptcy.

1895   Mark went on a worldwide tour to clear
        his debts. While travelling, his daughter
        Susy died.

1896   He published *Personal Recollections of Joan of
        Arc* under the name Sieur Louis de Conte.
        He based his descriptions of Joan of Arc
        on his daughter, Susy.

1901   Mark received an Honorary Doctor of
        Letters degree from Yale University.

1904   Mark's wife Olivia died. He moved
        to New York City to write his
        autobiography – the story of his life.

1907   He received an Honorary Doctor of
        Letter degree from Oxford University.

1908   Mark moved to Redding, Connecticut. A
        year later, his youngest daughter Jean died.

1910   Mark died in his home at the age of 74.

Jacques Prévert

◆ ◆ ◆

1900–1977

the Frenchman who is known as
'the People's Poet'

**When I was a young man, I saw the people of France
live through the horrors of war and terrible disease. I
saw them suffering and I wanted to write about them. I
wrote my poems, songs and later, my <u>screenplays</u> for the
people I loved – the French.**

◆ ◆ ◆

I was born on 4ᵗʰ February 1900 in France, in Neuilly-sur-
Seine, near the centre of Paris. I had two brothers, one older
and one younger, and I had a happy childhood. My father
worked for the Central Office for the Poor of Paris and
often took me with him when he was visiting the poorer,
<u>working-class</u> areas of the city. From a very young age I felt
a kind of sympathy for the people we saw there. My own
family belonged to the <u>middle classes</u>, a group of society
that had a set of social behaviours, and rules that you were
expected to follow and obey. I thought many of these were

just ridiculous and in general I did not see why I had to obey anything.

My father also wrote reviews of plays for the local newspapers and he often took me and my brothers to the theatre – something that I always enjoyed. I went to school until the age of 14, when I decided that I didn't want any more formal education and I left. It was also the year – 1914 – that the First World War began.

The world had never seen a war like this one before. By the time it was over we referred to it as The Great War as nobody could imagine that in less than 25 years, another World War would take place. On the one side were the Central Powers: Germany, Austria-Hungary, and the <u>Ottoman Empire</u> and on the other, the Allied Powers: Great Britain, France, Russia, Italy, Japan and later in 1917, the USA. The causes were many and were very complex, but the effect was simple – death and destruction that can only be described as <u>horrific</u>. In the four years the war lasted, more than 8.5 million soldiers were killed and 1.3 million of them were French. Most of them were young men, just three or four years older than I was.

◆ ◆ ◆

I was too young to join the army and fight. Instead, I got a job in a large department store in the centre of Paris called Bon Marché. I did all sorts of little jobs – took messages from one department to another, carried parcels, packets and boxes and did whatever I was told to do. I had not liked school and for me this was better than sitting in a classroom. Also, I was paid. It wasn't a lot of money but it was important. The biggest benefit was that I was learning about the real world. I learnt a great deal about human behaviour from the customers and I learnt even more about the value of money and what it can buy.

In 1918, when I was 18, I went to do my military service, which every young man in France had to do. So far, not many French soldiers had survived the war and, in addition to the dead, more than four million young Frenchmen had been wounded. Naturally, I was very anxious about being sent off to fight, but on 11th November 1918, the war ended when the peace agreement – the armistice – was signed.

In the spring of 1918, a new and more dangerous threat attacked the world. It was called Spanish Influenza. This was a terrible disease that turned into a huge epidemic, killing its victims in just a few days. The strange thing about it was that strong healthy young people seemed to catch it – and die from it – more easily than any other group of people. Far more people – millions more – died of this than had died in the war and there was nothing that doctors could do to stop it or treat it. I was lucky and did not become ill.

At the beginning of my military service, I was sent to Lunéville in eastern France. Here I became friends with a man called Yves Tanguy who later became a surrealist painter. Then in 1921, I was sent to Turkey, to Constantinople – Istanbul, as it was later called – and I made friends with another man, Marcel Duhamel.

◆ ◆ ◆

On my return from military service in 1922, I began to write short stories. I rented a flat with Marcel on Rue du Château, a street in Montparnasse which had become popular with artists of different kinds. Yves Tanguy came to join us, and free of the discipline and control of army life, we started to enjoy ourselves. We made friends with artists, poets and writers, spending most of our time in the cafés of our neighbourhood and we led a bohemian lifestyle. This meant that we did not like the social rules we were supposed to follow and we were not interested in money and what it could buy. Of course we had to have enough money to live on, so Marcel got a job as a hotel manager and with his salary, the three of us – and our friends – managed perfectly well.

We started to follow a new philosophical approach to art, and to life in general, called Surrealism. We believed that the subconscious mind – the part of the brain that influences you even though you are not aware of it – is where a person's imagination is. Most of the time, we cannot access our imagination because our conscious mind is worried about what society says we can and cannot do. As a result, it blocks us from listening to what the subconscious – and our imagination – is trying to tell us. If you can clear your subconscious mind, you will discover a whole new world of artistic and literary talent. Surrealism was heavily influenced by the work of <u>Sigmund Freud</u> and <u>Karl Marx</u>.

Together with our friends, who were artists, writers and people who wanted political change, we were reacting against France's recent history – of its human disasters in the Great War and of the Spanish flu epidemic – and it showed in our behaviour. Our actions were influenced by emotion instead of reason. Often we did not think before doing something and we were far more interested in experiencing life rather than learning about it. We were a group that valued a person's opinions and rights. We strongly believed that everyone had the right to follow their dreams and also to challenge those in power. After all, the politicians and military people had caused the Great War. We didn't like religion, either, nor the priests who represented it. We met in cafés and in our flat, convincing ourselves that the new society we dreamed of was the only possible way of life. Our friend, André Breton, wrote the *Surrealist Manifesto* in 1925, turning our revolutionary ideas into a real philosophy.

As I sat in the cafés of Paris, I got ideas for many stories. For example, there was a man who used to sit in a café for hour after hour. No one talked to him, as he looked like a homeless person. He was dressed in rough dirty clothes and no one wanted to know him. Who was this poor-looking man? I imagined him as being the last man to return from the Great War. His family was dead and he had no friends, for they were killed in the fighting. He sat in the café and waited for the day to pass, slowly drinking his coffee, trying to recover from his injuries. He was afraid and lonely.

I wanted to write about normal people, painting with words the scenes of the day and capturing, for a moment in time, their lives. I didn't know most of them, but I tried to reflect their hopes and fears. I was a poet of the café, the street, the war, and the community – a voice for those who had little influence. There were other people who walked past me as I sat in the cafés, who said little, but knew a lot. Who were those people and what were their stories? Where did they come from and where did they go to? These were questions that fascinated me. I wanted to write stories about people trying to beat despair and misery. Some of them were people who realized that, for various reasons, life was short. Others were those who were doing their best to stay normal after witnessing the madness and horror of war. They were people trying to make new relationships when their friends and family had gone. These were the stories of Paris and France.

◆ ◆ ◆

One of our large group of friends was a woman called Simone Dienne. She and I fell in love and we got married in 1925. This may sound strange as we did not believe in social rules like marriage, but for some reason, it was something that we wanted to do, and our marriage lasted for ten years. I spent the next few years sitting in cafés, watching people and getting ideas for my stories and poems.

In 1928, Yves, Marcel and I quarrelled with André Breton – who by this time had become our leader – and André left the group. I found a job in a company that made advertisements and spent my time writing poetry. My first poems were published in the early 1930s. In 1932, I joined a theatre group called Groupe Octobre which had connections to the <u>Communist Party</u>. I wrote plays for them using surrealist ideas and language, and they contained strong political messages. With my younger brother, Pierre, I wrote a play called *The Affair is in the Bag*, and the following year, in 1933, I went to Moscow, where my play *The Battle of Fontenoy* was being performed for the first time at the International Workers' Theatre Olympiad.

The world of theatre was a world of fantasy, love and passion but the new medium of film was beginning to give wider opportunities. I met the film makers Jean Renoir and Marcel Carné while I was with Groupe Octobre and we produced a number of films. With Renoir, I wrote a film called *Le crime de Monsieur Lange* and then I worked with Carné on the film *Jenny*, which was the beginning of a long working relationship. In 1936, Groupe Octobre broke up. Left-wing politics in France and Europe was changing and we were no longer sure how or where we fitted in. At this time I wrote a poem called *La Crosse en l'air*.

Carné and I started making films that had a big impact on French cinema. Films like *Bizarre, Bizarre* and *Port of Shadows* were categorized as being 'poetic realism', a type of film that had not been made before. This new type of film also had some influence in Hollywood, where the first films of the type called 'film noir' were being made. These were films by directors like Orson Welles, Billy Wilder and Alfred Hitchcock. They were often crime stories and had complex plots, many flashbacks and featured dramatic lighting techniques.

◆ ◆ ◆

In 1939, the Second World War started and the following year, France was invaded by Nazi Germany. Many of my colleagues and friends were arrested — some of them disappeared and were never seen again. I decided I would move to the south of France and went to stay in a place called Saint-Paul-de-Vence. Here I continued making films. In 1944, Carné directed a film that I had written the script for called *Les Enfants du Paradis* (Children of Paradise). It received good reviews then and later it was even said to be one of the best films ever produced.

In the meantime, I had not stopped writing poetry. In 1945, when the war ended, I published a book of poems called *Paroles*, which to my great surprise was a huge success. Half a million copies were sold in France – more than any book of poetry had sold before. My poems appealed to the new generation who had grown up during the German <u>occupation</u> of France and were finding it difficult to understand how the church and government fitted into their lives. The poems in *Paroles* were made even more popular when they were turned into songs by the Hungarian composer Joseph Kosma, who had written the music for some of the films I had produced. Two of the most popular singers in France at the time, Yves Montand and Juliette Greco sang and recorded *Autumn Leaves*, which was probably the most famous of all my poems.

Then I started working with the cartoonist Paul Grimault, who had also been a member of Groupe Octobre, and we produced several <u>animated</u> films such as *The Little Soldier*, which was released in 1947. I worked with Paul on different projects for the rest of my life and he was one of my best friends. At the time of my death, we had been working on a film called *The King and the Mockingbird*. On the night that the film was first shown, three years after my death, Paul kept the seat next to him empty.

◆ ◆ ◆

1948 was not a good year for me. Firstly, my working relationship with Marcel Carné ended when a film we were working on was cancelled in the middle of production. Then, I fell down some stairs and was seriously ill. I was in a <u>coma</u> for several weeks but fortunately, I recovered. By this time, I had remarried. My second wife was called Janine Loris and she had also been a member of Groupe Octobre. When I was released from hospital, we went back to live in Saint-Paul-de-Vence but in 1955, we came back to Paris. I was now so well-known that people sometimes stopped me in the street, speaking lines of my poems. In 1957, a film was made called *The Seine Meets Paris* and my poetry formed the basis of the script. My next period of creativity resulted in a series of art <u>collages</u>. In 1957, an exhibition was held in Paris with 60 of my collages, and then in Antibes in the south of France there was another exhibition of collages in 1963.

In 1973, my last book of poems was published. It was called *Things and Other Things*. At around that time, I felt the need to live in a cleaner atmosphere with fresh air as I was experiencing difficulties with my breathing. My wife and I went to live in a small village in Normandy called Omonville-la-Petite, where I died on 11th April 1977. Our house was next to a farm and not far from the village church and it was from there that I looked back on my life and ideas. My writing mixed the surreal with words from the street. The street is where I was happiest, listening to the stories of real people in the cafés and recording my <u>perceptions</u> of their needs and dreams. Yes, to be the people's poet was my <u>destiny</u> in life.

The Life of Jacques Prévert

1900   Jacques Prévert was born in Neuilly-sur-Seine, France on 4th February 1900. He was the second of three sons.

1914   The Germans invaded France in the First World War.

1915   Jacques finished school and began working in the department store Bon Marché.

1918   He began his military service in the French Army, but on 11th November, an armistice was signed and Jacques was sent elsewhere in Europe.

1921   He became friends with Marcel Duhamel while serving in Istanbul, Turkey.

1922   Jacques returned to Paris, and moved into a flat with Marcel on Rue du Château, a street in the artistic Montparnasse neighbourhood of Paris. That soon became the meeting place of the surrealist circle led by André Breton.

1925   Jacques married Simone Dienne.

c. 1928   The Rue du Château surrealist group broke up after a disagreement. Jacques began working for a company that made advertisements and writing poetry.

1931   One of his first poems, *Tentative de description d'un dîner de têtes à Paris-France* was published.

1932   He joined the left-wing Groupe Octobre, where he met film-maker Jean Renoir. They worked together on a large number of productions.

1936   With changes in the French and European left-wing politics, Groupe Octobre broke up. Jacques' poem *La Crosse en l'air* was published. He began working with film director Marcel Carné on the film *Jenny*, which was the beginning of a successful partnership.

1940   Following the Nazi invasion of France, Jacques moved south to Saint-Paul-de-Vence.

1944   The film *Les Enfants du Paradis* (Children of Paradise) was released. Jacques had written the script. It was considered one of the best movies of cinema history.

1945   His collection of poems *Paroles* was published, which made him France's most popular poet of the twentieth century.

1948   Jacques' partnership with film director
Marcel Carné ended after their film
La Fleur de l'age was cancelled during
production. Then Jacques spent some
weeks in a coma after a serious fall.
Following his recovery, he moved back to
Saint-Paul-de-Vence with his second wife,
Janine Loris.

1955   His work became enormously popular in
France, and he moved back to Paris.

1957   An exhibition of 60 of his art collages was
held in Paris.

1963   Another exhibition was held in Antibes,
Southern France.

1977   Jacques died at his home in Omonville-
La-Petite, Normandy, France. On the
same day, film director Marcel Carné was
quoted as calling him 'the one and only
poet of French cinema'.

Ayn Rand

♦ ♦ ♦

1905–1982

the writer who created the philosophy
of Objectivism

When I was a young girl in Russia, I saw the first films being shown. From that time I knew that I wanted to write stories that could be made into movies. I moved to the USA and I managed to turn my dream into reality.

◆ ◆ ◆

I was born in Saint Petersburg, Russia, on 2nd February 1905. My parents, Zinovy and Anna Rosenbaum, named me Alisa Zinov'yevna Rosenbaum but I later changed my name to Ayn Rand and that is how I am known today. I came from a <u>middle-class</u> <u>Jewish</u> family and my father was a pharmacist with his own shop. <u>Tsar</u> Nicholas II was in power. He was a <u>dictator</u> who did not like Jews, which sometimes made life difficult for us. In 1911, we moved to an apartment on a street called Nevsky Prospekt which was, and still is, one of the main streets of St Petersburg. Our street was close to Znamenskaya Square, which was renamed Vasstaniya Square after the Revolution. I learnt to read when I was quite young and by the age of 8, in 1913, I knew I wanted to be a writer and write <u>screenplays</u> for films.

The following year, the First World War began. The newspapers were full of horror stories and told of the millions of people who were being killed across Europe. Russian soldiers were also fighting and, as an increasing amount of money was needed for the army, our standard of living declined. The <u>working classes</u> in Russia had been unhappy for many years. Their working conditions were terrible and they were not being paid enough money to survive.

In 1917, towards the end of the First World War, poor people, angry and tired of living in poverty and seeing no change, crowded into the cities. Fighting broke out and bitter battles were fought as a <u>civil war</u> in Russia, or the Russian Revolution as it was also called, began. The result was that in 1917, the <u>Communists</u> gained power in Russia. Vladimir Lenin and his men took over from the hated Tsar, but I doubted if the new rulers would be any better. Until then, my father had been successful in business. He owned a pharmacy and with the income he had bought a building. All that changed when the Communists gained power.

My father's business was <u>confiscated</u> and we had to leave. We went to Crimea in the hope that we would be able to make money again but conditions were no better there and in 1921, we returned to Saint Petersburg, which had been renamed Petrograd.

In the meantime, I had been getting an education and I graduated from high school in 1921 before we left Crimea. I was a good student and found school easy. Apart from writing, I particularly liked mathematics. In 1915, when I was 10 years old, I had written my first novel. When we came back to Saint Petersburg, the city was in a state of great confusion as nobody knew what was going to happen in the near future. Jobs were hard to find and we almost <u>starved</u> while we were trying to find paid work. The revolution had one benefit, though. The universities had been told to open their doors to women and I was one of the first women to enrol. I studied philosophy and history and also took courses in French and German. The philosophers Aristotle and Plato made a major impression on my thinking, as did the work of Friedrich Nietzsche.

I was not in favour of our new Communist society. I saw that it did not allow people the freedom to express what they thought and it became obvious that discrimination and <u>corruption</u> were still very much present. In 1924, a group of students, myself included, were forced to leave the university because the government thought we were 'bourgeois' – in other words, we belonged to the conventional middle classes. A group of visiting scientists made a formal request to the government to allow us back into the university. They were successful, and we were we able to complete our studies. I graduated in 1924 and decided to go to the State Institute for Cinema Art for a year to study how to write screenplays. I wrote a short book called *Hollywood: American Movie City*, which was published.

◆ ◆ ◆

In 1925, when I was 20 years old, I wanted to explore the world. I also wanted to escape from the lack of artistic and <u>intellectual</u> freedom in Russia. I had relatives in the USA who invited me to visit them and luckily I was given permission to leave Russia. It was at this time that I chose to change my name and I became Ayn Rand. The train journey across Europe was an adventure and the voyage on the Atlantic Ocean took me to a whole new world.

In 1926, New York, in contrast to Petrograd, was full of people moving about freely and saying what they wanted, without fear of being arrested. Private property was respected, too. There were many other foreigners and I immediately felt comfortable. I went to Chicago and stayed with my relatives. Living with them helped me to learn English quickly. One of them owned a cinema and I watched the films for free, which also helped me learn the language. From the start, I wrote down my observations and ideas.

I was determined to have my career as a writer and so I went to Hollywood. To pay the bills, I took several low paid part-time jobs until one day I met the film director, Cecil B. DeMille. He gave me first a minor non-speaking role in a film he was making called *The King of Kings* and then a job as a junior writer. I knew from that time that I wanted to stay in America. While I was working on *The King of Kings*, I met an actor called Frank O'Connor. We enjoyed each other's company and started spending time together. Before long, he asked me to marry him. We got engaged and on 15th April 1929, we got married.

I was now living the life that I had dreamed about. Frank introduced me to many people and I got a job working in the costume department for RKO Studios. In 1929, while I was at RKO, a huge economic crash occurred, which had a terrible effect all over the world. Millions of people became unemployed and the streets were full of people begging for money or food. I was one of the lucky ones.

I wrote every day and my ability to write in English improved greatly. A screenplay I had written called *Red Pawn* was sold to Universal Studios in 1932. Despite the fact that it was never made into a film, my name became well-known in the film industry. It was a time when ideas for plays and novels came to me as well as for other films.

◆ ◆ ◆

My family regularly sent news from Russia. Before I left, Vladimir Lenin had died in 1924. He had been replaced by Joseph Stalin and things began to change for the people of Russia. The Communist Party controlled every part of their daily lives. The working classes had been promised freedom but now they lived in fear. Large numbers of people were arrested regularly as Russia was under the iron fist of Stalin and his government – the Kremlin.

In 1931, I gained US citizenship and my first thought was to ask my parents to join me. Despite many efforts, permission was not given. Russia, under the Communists, became like a giant prison as its citizens were locked in and most foreigners were kept out. Although we continued to write to each other, I never saw my parents again.

Writing became a way of life for me. In 1934, I wrote a play called *Ideal* and the first film I wrote the screenplay for, called *Woman on Trial*, was released. In the same year, I moved to New York. In 1936, a play I had written four years before called *Night of January 16th*, was performed on Broadway. Next, a book which was partly based on my own life, called *We the Living* was finally published. It had taken me several years to find a publisher who would accept it. It was about the difficult and <u>harsh</u> life that people in Russia were experiencing because of the communist government, and it reflected the ideas of Aristotle that I was so fond of.

In 1939, the Second World War began. The Germans had once again attacked their European neighbours and before long, they invaded Russia. The aim of the <u>Nazis</u> was to kill all Jews and I feared for my family. After our last exchange of letters just before the war, I never heard from them again and never knew what had happened to them. I reflected on my wise decision to live in the USA.

In 1940, Frank and I supported the <u>Republican</u> candidate Wendell Willkie in his campaign to become president. At about that time my play, *The Unconquered*, opened on Broadway. In 1941, the Japanese bombed Pearl Harbor in Hawaii, which was an American state. Previously the Second World War had involved only Europe, but now that the USA was involved, it had become a global conflict. To keep my mind on work, I wrote a number of screenplays. A novel I had written in 1935 called *The Fountainhead* was published – although it had been rejected by 12 publishers previously – and in 1943, I sold the film rights to Warner Brothers. I wrote the screenplay for the film starring Gary Cooper and Patricia Neil, which made a lot of money.

I began receiving letters from readers who were influenced by my writing and we formed a group which met regularly to discuss philosophy. One of the members of the group, a man called Nathaniel Branden, was a <u>psychologist</u> and he became a special friend to me. In 1944, Frank and I moved to the San Fernando Valley in southern California where we bought a house. I was extremely busy writing. In 1945, I wrote the screenplays for two films: *Love Letters* and *You*

New York City

Came Along. It was also a time where seriously hard work was necessary to complete projects and I became addicted to a medicine which I had been given by my doctor to stop me feeling tired. Later my addiction seriously affected my health.

In 1951, I moved back to New York and in 1957 I published a book called *Atlas Shrugged*, which featured a group of strong-minded characters, with a determination to win in life. *Atlas Shrugged* summed up the main ideas of a kind of philosophy I started, which was later called Objectivism. It was based on the beliefs of Aristotle, and the ideas of self-interest and self-responsibility. We should live our lives using rational thoughts, based on reason rather than emotion, and actions based on the truth. My friend Nathaniel started the Nathaniel Branden Institute (NBI) which supported Objectivism.

I argued that people's self-interest should be allowed to grow and develop. My view was that we have <u>free will</u>, but institutions like the church prevent it. Politics and laws should support free choice – each person should be able to decide what they want to do with their life. Taxation, used to control people, should no longer exist, and free competition should be encouraged, as it allows the best people to succeed. Many people said my views supported the business culture of the USA. I continued writing. In 1961, I published the book, *For The New Intellectual* and in 1962, the first issue of *The Objectivist Newsletter* was published. I was given an <u>honorary doctorate</u> from Lewis and Clark University in 1963. Also, I spoke at many conferences in a controversial way. I <u>opposed</u> the Vietnam War and compulsory military service and I supported women's rights. In 1964, I published a book called *The Virtue of Selfishness* and I spent the next few years deeply involved in teaching and writing.

◆ ◆ ◆

In 1968, my friendship with Nathaniel ended. I started teaching a course about writing non-fiction. In 1979, my husband Frank died. I kept on talking and publishing and in 1981, I spoke at my last lecture in New Orleans. By this time, my health was suffering badly. I had been smoking heavily for many years and I was having difficulty breathing properly. On 6th March 1982, I died at my home in New York. I was 77 years old. My life had been a series of contrasts. I had lived in poverty in Russia and had become a millionaire in the USA. I had experienced lack of freedom in communist Russia and enjoyed <u>capitalism</u> in the USA. But I had lived and acted out my own philosophy of life. I had been free to choose my own path to happiness.

The Life Of Ayn Rand

1905   Ayn was born in Saint Petersburg, Russia. Her parents named her Alisa Zinov'yevna Rosenbaum.

1911–1912   Ayn learnt to read very early in her life. Her family moved to an apartment on Nevsky Prospekt at Znamenskaya Square.

1913   Aged 8, she began writing screenplays. Around this time, she decided to become a writer.

1914   The First World War started, which had an impact on the standard of living.

1915   At the age of 10, Ayn was writing novels.

1917   The Russian Revolution began.

1918   Ayn's family moved to Crimea to escape the civil war.

1921   She graduated from Yevpatoria High School in Crimea. Her family returned to Petrograd (the new name for Saint Petersburg), where Ayn enrolled at the State University.

1924   Ayn graduated from the University and enrolled at the State Technicum for Screen Arts, where she studied writing for films for a year.

1925   Ayn was granted a visa to visit her relatives in the USA. Around that time, she also adopted her literary name, Ayn Rand.

1926   Ayn's booklet *Hollywood: American Movie City* was published. She went to the United States and lived with her relatives in Chicago. She moved to Hollywood and was hired by Cecil B. DeMille to appear in a film. She also met the actor Frank O'Connor.

1927   She was hired by Cecil B. DeMille as a junior screen writer.

1929   Ayn married Frank O'Connor. She worked at RKO Studios. The economic crash occurred.

1931   She became an American citizen.

1932   Universal Studios bought her screenplay *Red Pawn*. However, it was never produced.

1934   Ayn wrote a play called *Ideal*. The film using her first screenplay, *Woman on Trial*, opened in Hollywood. Ayn moved to New York City.

1935   Her play *Night of January 16th* was shown for the first time.

1936   Ayn's first novel *We the Living*, which was partly based on her life, was published.

1938   Her short book *Anthem* was published.

1939   She received the last letters from her family in the USSR. The Second World War began.

1940   Ayn and Frank supported the presidential campaign of Republican Wendell Willkie. Her play *The Unconquered* opened on Broadway.

1943   One of her best-selling novels, *The Fountainhead*, was published. She sold the film rights to Warner Brothers.

1944   Ayn and Frank moved to the San Fernando Valley.

1945   She wrote screenplays for *Love Letters* and *You Came Along*.

1951   She moved back to New York City.

1957   Ayn's longest novel, *Atlas Shrugged*, was published.

1958   She began teaching fiction writing classes. The Nathaniel Branden Institute (NBI) was opened to support Ayn's philosophy of 'Objectivism'.

1960   She gave her first major talk at Yale University.

1961   The book *For the New Intellectual* was published.

1962   The first issue of *The Objectivist Newsletter* was published.

1963   Ayn received an honorary doctorate from Lewis & Clark University.

1964   *The Virtue of Selfishness* was published.

1966   *Capitalism: The Unknown Ideal* was published. The first part of *Introduction to Objectivist Epistemology* was published in *The Objectivist Newsletter*.

1968–1969   *The Romantic Manifesto* was published. She began teaching a non-fiction writing course.

1971   Ayn published *The New Left: The Anti-Industrial Revolution*.

1979   Ayn's husband Frank died.

1981   She gave her last public lecture, *The Sanction of the Victims*, in New Orleans.

1982   Ayn published *Philosophy: Who Needs It*. She died aged 77, at her home in New York City, USA.

Aleksandr Solzhenitsyn

◆ ◆ ◆

1918–2008

the author who wrote about life in a
Soviet Labour Camp

I grew up in a place where it was dangerous to give your own opinion if it was different to that of the government. I was arrested and punished for something I wrote in a private letter to a friend.

◆ ◆ ◆

I was born on 11th December 1918, in Kislovodsk which was a fashionable spa town in Russia in between the Black Sea and the Caspian Sea. My parents named me Aleksandr Isayevich Solzhenitsyn. My father, Isaakiy, died six months before my birth. He was an officer in the army and although he survived four years' fighting in the First World War, he died in a hunting accident not long after he came home. I was brought up by my mother and aunt. My mother, Taisiya, was an educated woman who spoke fluent French and English and who worked as a typist. In 1924, when I was 6 years old, we moved to a place called Rostov-on-Don in south Russia and it was here that I grew up. In 1922, Russia became part of the USSR – the Union of Soviet Socialist Republics.

Like most children I believed what I was told. The Great Russian Revolution of 1917 would lead to a fairer society. The ideas of <u>Karl Marx</u> would guide our future now that <u>Communism</u> had replaced the rule of the <u>Tsars</u>. Lenin, our new leader, said the <u>slavery</u> of <u>serfdom</u> had ended. Everyone would be educated and a new age of equality would begin. But, how long would it take? By the time I was 10 years old in 1928, questions like this were being asked. Joseph Stalin had become the leader of Russia when Lenin died, but our living conditions were still poor. Many people were still without work, and without money they could not buy what they needed to survive, not even food. Hunger was a serious problem, as it made people weak and took away their energy. Our family was no exception and life was difficult.

We owned some property, but private property was not allowed. In 1930, it was taken from us and turned into a farm called a collective that was owned by the new Soviet Union. It was not possible to question the government as they used force to support their decisions. They told us that everyone had to work for the State, and that everyone was supposed to support each other. At the local school, I was told collectivization was good for our country, that it was necessary to establish equality. Equality, however, was not something we saw. It soon became clear that the hard work 'everyone' was doing was benefiting the people who worked in the government. They had nice houses, plenty of food and a good life. Ordinary people still had nothing – not even enough food to eat.

◆ ◆ ◆

I had decided as a young boy that I wanted to study literature and become a writer but at the University of Rostov-on-Don, literature was not one of the subjects they taught. We didn't have enough money to send me to Moscow to study, so in 1937, I enrolled at the university in my home town and I studied mathematics instead. It was possible, though, to do some 'distance learning' courses run by The Institute of History, Philosophy and Literature in Moscow, so two years later, I managed to study these subjects as well. Luckily I was good at mathematics, which later proved to be extremely useful and probably saved my life.

◆ ◆ ◆

In the meantime, the Second World War had started in 1939, when Adolf Hitler's army invaded Poland. In the beginning, Stalin made an <u>alliance</u> with the <u>Nazis</u>. To me it seemed an unnatural alliance, as Stalin was suspicious of the Germans, and speeches made by the German leader, Hitler, suggested he was anti-<u>communist</u>. However, our leader, Stalin was surprised when the Germans invaded Russia in 1942 and the Russian army's defences were unprepared and weak. I had joined the army in 1941, after graduating from college, just a year after getting married. My wife, Natalya, was a chemistry student I had met at university. There were fierce battles, and I saw many good men die. I, myself, was fortunate to survive and I twice received medals for my actions in battle.

As the war continued, I began seriously to doubt the decisions our leaders were making. In particular, I felt Stalin had created many of the disasters that caused millions of our people to die. I was also upset with the danger Russian people were facing from the secret police. This was an organization set up by the government to secretly control people who were political enemies. We had been told about the threats that foreign countries presented, but I thought our secret police was worse. Anyone who openly disagreed with Communism disappeared and was often never seen again. During the war when I was far away from home, I wrote letters to my friends. In one letter I criticized Joseph Stalin and expressed my doubts about his skills as a leader. Unfortunately, my letter was read by someone with connections to the secret police and I was arrested and taken to the much-feared Lubyanka Prison in Moscow.

Here I was questioned repeatedly about spreading anti-Soviet <u>propaganda</u> and then after the questions, I was beaten. Despite denying the charges, I was found guilty on 7th July 1945 – although I was not present at my own trial – and I was sentenced to spend eight years in a Soviet Labour Camp. This was a type of prison. The criminals' punishment was to do hard physical work for many hours each day. The conditions inside the camps were terrible and cruel. An eight-year sentence was, at that time, not a very strict punishment. This was Stalin's way of silencing any <u>opposition</u>. He himself had been sent to a labour camp twice, when he was a revolutionary before the communists took power, so he knew all about life in the camps or 'katorgas' as they were known. He survived, though, and I decided I would do the same.

For the first five months, I was sent to work on a series of building projects near Moscow. Then because of my mathematics background, I was sent to a scientific research centre, where I spent the next four years. In 1950, I was sent to a new kind of camp, a 'Special Camp' for political prisoners. Our punishment was hard work and that was what we did. The days were long and the sentence seemed never ending. It was difficult in the summer heat, but it was far, far worse in the bitter cold of the winter. I was a young man – not a very healthy young man – but I could cope with the physical difficulties better than some of the other prisoners. We were called *zeks*, which means 'prisoners'. We did different types of work, but whatever we did, we were really just slaves.

While I was in the Special Camp, I became ill with cancer and had an operation to remove a <u>tumour</u>. I thought it was funny that they wanted to save me so that I could be punished some more. In 1952, my marriage ended as it was too difficult for Natalya to continue being married to me. The following year, I completed the eight years I had been sentenced to and was expecting to be allowed to go home. This did not happen. A decision was made, far away in some government office without my knowledge and without a review of my case, to <u>exile</u> me for life. It wasn't a personal decision – many other prisoners were affected as well. I was sent to Kok-Terek, in southern Kazakhstan.

◆ ◆ ◆

In 1953, I became very ill again because of the cancer that had not been cured by the first operation or properly identified by the doctors, and I nearly died. I was taken to hospital again in the city of Tashkent, Uzbekistan, and this time, my treatment was successful. While lying in bed, I thought about the years since I had graduated from university. I had served my country well in war but I had been rejected by my country's leaders. I asked myself why this had happened.

I was not guilty of any criminal offence but in the minds of Russian leaders, I was seen as a threat. I did not believe in <u>Marxism</u>, Communism or <u>Stalinism</u> but certain <u>principles</u> did make sense to me, such as, 'Behave to others in a way that you would like them to behave towards you.' These thoughts made me want to write but I could not do so while I was in the camp. Instead of actually putting pen to paper, I 'thought' stories and poems and memorized them. I had written 28 poems in this way while I was in the *gulags* – that is the name we gave to the <u>harsh</u> prison camps. My creativity helped the time to pass and give meaning to my life.

Another four years passed before I was released from exile. Stalin had died in 1953, but it took time for change to occur. In 1956, at the age of 38, I returned home and found work as a maths teacher. The following year, Natalya and I got married again and this time we stayed married until 1972. Each evening, I returned to my apartment and wrote. I did not really have any expectation that my books would ever be published, but putting my experiences on paper was good for me. I also thought that I had a duty to record what had happened to me and thousands of other political prisoners. There was so much to say about the justice system and the work camps but I was afraid to show my work to anyone in case I was imprisoned again. Apart from being afraid, I was also feeling <u>frustrated</u> that my work was not being seen by anyone in the literary world. I decided this situation had to change.

In November 1962, surprisingly, one of my books was accepted for publication. The title was *One Day in the Life of Ivan Denisovich* and it appeared in the Soviet literary magazine *Novy Mir*. It was about what it was like to be in the labour camps and this was the first time most people could read about them. Almost as soon as printing started, the government stopped it. But, again to my surprise, many international publishers found my work, had it translated and published, and my name started to be known abroad. The secret police, whose name had become the KGB, watched me as they knew I was someone who was against the government.

Even though I was afraid, I kept writing – late at night, and hiding the manuscripts, as I had done before when I was writing *One Day in the Life of Ivan Denisovich*. *The Gulag Archipelago* was written between 1958 and 1968, although it wasn't published until 1973. It described, in three books of detail, the terrible camps and in particular, how good men and women were falsely imprisoned. However, one day in 1965 the secret police entered my apartment by force and searched it. They found nothing, but the KGB agents arrested my typist and took her away. They <u>tortured</u> her until she told them where my papers were. Within days of her release, she was found hanged.

I made new arrangements with friends to hide my work. Heli Susi, a friend's daughter, bravely took my writings to Estonia. My other form of protection was provided by a friend, who was called Mstislav Rostropovich. He was a world-famous musician and this gave him some privacy. He invited me to stay at his *dacha* – his holiday house in the country – and that is where I worked. In 1968, I wrote the books *Cancer Ward* and then *The First Circle*, which described my experiences at a prison for scientists.

◆ ◆ ◆

In 1970, I was awarded the Nobel Prize in Literature, but I did not travel to Sweden to receive it, as there was a danger the Russian Government would exile me again. Having been exiled once was enough. In 1971, my book about The First World War, *August 1914*, was published. In 1973, the first of my three books describing the <u>horrific</u> camps, *The Gulag Archipelago*, was published. In the same year, I married a woman called Natalia Svetlova and we went on to have three sons.

I was now quite famous all over the world for writing about my experiences. But the Russian government did not want people to learn about what I had to say. On 12th February 1974, I was arrested and the next day I was made to leave Russia and was sent to Frankfurt, Germany. My Russian citizenship was taken away from me. Natalia and I needed some peace in our lives and we decided to go and live in Switzerland. I felt safe for the first time since my youth. We had our three sons and life was busy.

While I was living there, an invitation arrived from the USA. Academics at the University of Stanford asked me to join them. We boarded a plane for a country which Russians regarded as an enemy. From the land of Communism, I was escaping to the land of <u>Capitalism</u> – something that I been told all my life was evil and full of <u>corruption</u>. The <u>Cold War</u> was at its peak with both the USSR and the USA having enough nuclear weapons to blow up the world.

◆ ◆ ◆

My reception at the Hoover Institution at the University of Stanford was warm, a contrast to life in Russia. It was the start of 17 years of a new life, even though I was focussing on the past. My research was on the Russian Revolution of 1917. I was a victim, like so many who were supposed to have benefited from it. In 1990, my Russian citizenship was finally given back to me and four years later, I returned to my native country, with my wife. I was 76 years old. We lived in a *dacha* near Moscow and before I died at the age of 89 in 2008, I had time to write and look back on my life.

I had seen the worst and the best of people and places. Deprived of my liberty, I had been a prisoner and an exile. It was strange because these were the experiences that gave me fame. Would I have won a Nobel Prize without the pain of prison? Even though I had been married twice, I saw little of family life. Making the best of your life is all you can do. Surviving to tell the world was a bonus.

The Life of Aleksandr Solzhenitsyn

1918   Aleksandr Isayevich Solzhenitsyn was born in Kislovodsk, Russia. His father died six months before his birth.

1924   Aleksandr and his mother moved to Rostov-on-Don.

1930   Their family property was taken away from them and turned into a collective farm.

1937   Aleksandr began to study in the Department of Physics and Mathematics at the University of Rostov-on-Don.

1939   He studied by distance learning at the Institute of History, Philosophy and Literature in Moscow.

1940   While at university, Aleksandr married Natalya Reshetovskaya.

1941   Aleksandr served in the Second World War in the Red Army.

1944   His mother died.

1945   While serving in the Red Army, he was arrested for criticizing Joseph Stalin in a letter to a friend. He was sent to a Soviet Labour Camp in Kazakhstan for eight years.

1946   Being a mathematician, he was taken out of the Labour camp and sent to a scientific research institute. During that time, he taught mathematics.

1950   Aleksandr was sent to a camp for political prisoners, where he did different kinds of work. While there, he developed cancer and was operated on but not cured.

1952   With prison life proving difficult for married life, Aleksandr and Natalya divorced a year before his release.

1953   After his sentence was over, Aleksandr was sent to internal exile for life at Kok-Terek in southern Kazakhstan. His cancer developed quickly and became life-threatening.

1954   He was sent to a cancer clinic in Tashkent, and was cured.

1956   Following Stalin's death, Aleksandr was freed from exile. After his return to Russia, he taught mathematics at a secondary school during the day and spent his nights secretly engaged in writing.

1957   Aleksandr remarried Natalya. However, their marriage ended in 1972.

1962   *One Day in the Life of Ivan Denisovich* was published. It was based upon Aleksandr's experiences in the labour camp. The book brought him immediate recognition. The printing was stopped, almost immediately, by the authorities.

1965   Aleksandr's manuscripts and private papers were <u>confiscated</u> by secret police.

1968   *The Cancer Ward* and *The First Circle* were published.

1970   Aleksandr was announced as winner of the Nobel Prize for Literature. However, he could not claim the prize due to his fear of being exiled again.

1971   Based on the First World War, *August 1914* was published.

1973   The first volume of *The Gulag Archipelago* was published. Two more books in the series followed, and described the terrible camps in detail.

1973   Aleksandr married Natalia Svetlova. They had three sons, Yermolai, Stepan and Ignat. His Russian citizenship was taken away from him. He and his family moved to Germany, then Switzerland, before finally moving to Cavendish, Vermont, USA.

1978   Aleksandr was given an <u>honorary</u> Literary Degree from Harvard University.

1989   *The Gulag Archipelago* was published in the literary magazine *Novy Mir.*

1994   After getting his citizenship back in 1990, Aleksandr returned home and settled with his family near Moscow.

1997   The Solzhenitsyn Prize for Russian writing was established in his honour.

2008   Aleksandr died aged 89, at his home near Moscow, Russia.

advisor COUNTABLE NOUN
An **advisor** is someone whose job is to advise important people on a particular subject.

alliance COUNTABLE NOUN
An **alliance** is an agreement between two countries, especially one in which they agree not to fight a war against each other but to be on the same side if there is a war.

Anglican ADJECTIVE
Anglican means belonging or relating to the Church of England, or to the churches related to it.

animated ADJECTIVE
An **animated** film is one in which puppets or drawings appear to move.

apprentice COUNTABLE NOUN
An **apprentice** is a person who works with someone in order to learn their skill.

aristocracy COUNTABLE NOUN
The **aristocracy** is a class of people in some countries who have a high social rank and special titles.

aristocratic ADJECTIVE
Aristocratic means belonging to or typical of the aristocracy.

bankruptcy UNCOUNTABLE NOUN
Bankruptcy is the state of being unable to pay your debts. If you **file for bankruptcy**, you ask a court to make you officially bankrupt, which means someone takes charge of your case and organizes your debts and repayments.

boarding school VARIABLE NOUN
A **boarding school** is a school where the pupils live during the term.

capitalism UNCOUNTABLE NOUN
Capitalism is an economic and political system in which property, business, and industry are owned by private individuals and not by the state.

Catholicism UNCOUNTABLE NOUN
Catholicism is the traditions, the behaviour, and the set of Christian beliefs that are held by members of the Catholic Church.

cause COUNTABLE NOUN
A **cause** is all the aims and objectives that a group of people are trying to achieve.

charity UNCOUNTABLE NOUN
Charity is the giving of money or other help to people who are poor and cannot manage on their own.

civil rights PLURAL NOUN
Civil rights are the rights that people have to equal treatment and equal opportunities, whatever their race, sex, or religion.

civil war COUNTABLE NOUN
A **civil war** is a war which is fought between different groups of people living in the same country.

Cold War PROPER NOUN
The Cold War was the period after the Second World War when relations between the Soviet Union and the countries in the West were very difficult, and the two groups did not cooperate in any way.

collage COUNTABLE NOUN
A **collage** is a picture made by sticking pieces of paper or cloth onto paper.

coma COUNTABLE NOUN
If someone is **in** a **coma**, they are deeply unconscious for a long time.

Communism UNCOUNTABLE NOUN
Communism is the political belief that all people are equal and that workers should control the means of producing things.

communist COUNTABLE NOUN
A **communist** is someone who supports a political system in which the state owns all property and controls the means of production, and everyone is supposed to be equal.
ADJECTIVE
Communist means relating to Communism.

Communist Party PROPER NOUN
The Communist Party is a political party that believes in Communism. There have been communist parties in many countries, and the Communist Party was the party of government in the USSR from 1917 to 1991.

Confederate Army PROPER NOUN
The Confederate Army was the army of the southern states who fought against the northern states in the American Civil War.

confiscate TRANSITIVE VERB
If people in authority **confiscate** something from someone, they take it away from them as a punishment or for political reasons.

corruption UNCOUNTABLE NOUN
Corruption is dishonesty and illegal behaviour by people in positions of power.

curate COUNTABLE NOUN
A **curate** is a priest in the Anglican Church whose job is to be an assistant to a more senior priest.

darkness UNCOUNTABLE NOUN
Darkness is an atmosphere of great sadness and unhappiness.

destiny SINGULAR NOUN
A person's **destiny** is everything that happens to them during their life, and that cannot be avoided.

dictator COUNTABLE NOUN
A **dictator** is a ruler who has complete power in a country, especially one who uses that power unfairly or cruelly.

doctorate COUNTABLE NOUN
A **doctorate** is the highest degree awarded by a university.

Doctor of Letters
COUNTABLE NOUN
A **Doctor of Letters** is someone who has been given the highest possible degree by a university because they have published a lot of work and done a lot of advanced research into a particular subject such as philosophy, literature, etc.

dwarf COUNTABLE NOUN
In children's stories, a **dwarf** is an imaginary creature that is like a small man. **Dwarfs** often have magical powers.

elite ADJECTIVE
An **elite** person or group is considered to be the best of their kind.

emperor COUNTABLE NOUN
An **emperor** is a man who rules an empire.

epidemic COUNTABLE NOUN
If there is an **epidemic** of a particular disease somewhere, it spreads quickly to a very large number of people there.

exile TRANSITIVE VERB
If someone **is exiled**, they have been sent out of their own country as a punishment and have to live in a foreign country.

UNCOUNTABLE NOUN
Exile is when someone has been sent out of their own country to live in a foreign country as a punishment. When this has happened, you can say that someone is living **in exile**.
COUNTABLE NOUN
An **exile** is someone who lives in exile.

flashback COUNTABLE NOUN
In a film, novel, or play, a **flashback** is a scene that involves events that happened earlier in the story.

free will UNCOUNTABLE NOUN
Free will is the ability that humans have to make decisions and choices without any outside influence.

frustrated ADJECTIVE
If you are **frustrated**, you are upset or annoyed by a problem that you cannot solve.

governess COUNTABLE NOUN
A **governess** is a woman who is employed by a family to live with them and educate their children.

gravity UNCOUNTABLE NOUN
Gravity is the invisible force which makes things fall when you drop them.

harsh ADJECTIVE
Harsh living conditions are very difficult for people to exist in.

honorary ADJECTIVE
Universities give **honorary** degrees to people who do not have the necessary formal qualifications, as a reward for the high standard of the work they have done in a particular field.

horrific ADJECTIVE
If you describe something as **horrific**, you mean that it is so bad that people are shocked by it and think it is disgusting.

imaginary ADJECTIVE
An **imaginary** person, place, or thing exists only in your mind or in a story, and not in real life.

imperialist ADJECTIVE
Imperialist activities involve a rich and powerful country trying to influence or take control of other countries.

influential ADJECTIVE
Someone who is **influential** has the power to control and influence other people or events.

injustice VARIABLE NOUN
Injustice is unfairness in a situation.

intellectual ADJECTIVE
Intellectual means involving a person's ability to think and to understand ideas and information.

Jewish ADJECTIVE
Jewish means belonging or relating to the religion of Judaism, which is based on the Old Testament of the Bible and the Talmud.

junction COUNTABLE NOUN
A **junction** is a place where roads or railway lines join.

Karl Marx PROPER NOUN
Karl Marx was a German philosopher and economist who developed the idea of communism. His two most famous books are *Das Kapital* and *The Communist Manifesto*. He died in 1883.

left-wing ADJECTIVE
Left-wing politics, groups, or ideas are based on the principles of socialism, whose general aim is to create a system in which everyone has an equal opportunity to benefit from a country's wealth.

logic UNCOUNTABLE NOUN
Logic is a way of thinking that involves reason rather than emotion.

Marxism UNCOUNTABLE NOUN
Marxism is a political philosophy based on the writings of Karl Marx, which stresses the importance of the struggle between different social classes.

middle class COUNTABLE NOUN
The middle class or **middle classes** are the people in a society who are not working class or upper class, for example managers, doctors, and lawyers.
ADJECTIVE
Middle-class people and families belong to the middle classes.

Midwest PROPER NOUN
The Midwest is the region in the north of the central part of the United States.

miner COUNTABLE NOUN
A **miner** is a person who works underground in mines in order to obtain minerals such as coal, silver, or gold.

Nazi COUNTABLE NOUN
The Nazis were members of the right-wing political party, led by Adolf Hitler, which held power in Germany from 1933 to 1945.
ADJECTIVE
You use **Nazi** to say that something relates to the Nazis.

occupation UNCOUNTABLE NOUN
The **occupation** of a country is its invasion and control by a foreign army.

official ADJECTIVE
Someone or something that is **official** is approved by the government or by someone else in authority.
COUNTABLE NOUN
An **official** is a person who holds a position of authority in an organization.

oppose TRANSITIVE VERB
If you **oppose** a course of action, you disagree with it and do not want to take part in it.

opposition UNCOUNTABLE NOUN
Opposition is strong disagreement with a plan or with a government, especially when it includes action to change or prevent a particular situation.

Ottoman Empire PROPER NOUN
The Ottoman Empire was an empire that began in Turkey in 1299 and lasted until 1922. It controlled most of south-east Europe, a lot of North Africa, and parts of the Middle East.

patriarch COUNTABLE NOUN
A **patriarch** is a man who is respected as the first or greatest leader of a group or society.

perception COUNTABLE NOUN
Your **perception of** something is the way that you think about it or the impression you have of it.

physicist COUNTABLE NOUN
A **physicist** is a person who studies physics, which is the science of matter and energy and the effects they have on each other.

plantation COUNTABLE NOUN
A **plantation** is a large area of land, where crops such as cotton, tea, or sugar are grown.

prayer COUNTABLE NOUN
A **prayer** is the words that someone says when they speak to God.

principal COUNTABLE NOUN
The **principal** of a school or college is the person in charge of it.

principle COUNTABLE NOUN
A **principle** is a belief that you have about the way you should behave.

propaganda UNCOUNTABLE NOUN
Propaganda is information, often inaccurate information, which is intended to influence people.

Protestant COUNTABLE NOUN
A **Protestant** is someone who belongs to the branch of the Christian church which separated from the Catholic church in the sixteenth century.

Prussia PROPER NOUN
Prussia was a powerful German state in northern and central Germany. When other German states joined with it in 1871, it became the leader of the German Empire. It was formally abolished in 1947.

psychologist COUNTABLE NOUN
A **psychologist** is a person who studies the human mind and tries to explain why people behave in the way that they do.

Republican COUNTABLE NOUN
In the United States, a **Republican** is a member of one of the two main political parties, called the Republican Party. It is more right-wing and conservative than the other party, which is called the Democratic party.

Royal Historiographer
PROPER NOUN
The Royal Historiographer is a historian who is appointed by a king or queen to write a history of a kingdom or of the royal family.

royalties PLURAL NOUN
Royalties are payments made to writers by publishers when their books are sold.

satirical ADJECTIVE
A **satirical** drawing or piece of writing criticizes something by using humour and by saying it is worse than it really is in order to make it look foolish or evil.

screenplay COUNTABLE NOUN
A **screenplay** is a script for a film, with all the words that the actors have to say.

serfdom UNCOUNTABLE NOUN
In Russia, **serfdom** was a system that lasted until 1861, in which most of the people who lived and worked in the countryside were owned by landowners.

share COUNTABLE NOUN
The **shares** of a company are the equal parts into which its ownership is divided. People who have shares in a company usually get some money from the company every year.

Sigmund Freud PROPER NOUN
Sigmund Freud was the first person to develop psychoanalysis, which is a way of treating people with mental problems by asking them about

their feelings and their past to establish the causes of their problems. He died in 1939.

slavery UNCOUNTABLE NOUN
Slavery is the state of being owned by other people as a slave.

Stalinism UNCOUNTABLE NOUN
Stalinism was the system of government used in the Soviet Union between 1928 and 1953 when Joseph Stalin was the leader of the country. It is characterized by the belief that there should only be one political party which controls everything, and that opposition parties should not be allowed.

starve INTRANSITIVE VERB
If people **starve**, they suffer a lot and die, or come close to dying, because they do not have enough food to eat.

steamboat COUNTABLE NOUN
A **steamboat** is a boat that has an engine which gets its power from steam.

surrealist ADJECTIVE
Surrealist means related to or in the style of surrealism, which is a type of art in which ideas, images, and objects combine in a strange way, like in a dream.

tactless ADJECTIVE
Someone who is **tactless** says or writes things that might offend other people, because they do not think carefully before they speak or write.

tobacco VARIABLE NOUN
Tobacco is a plant that grows in hot areas, and whose leaves are dried and used to make cigars and cigarettes.

tolerance UNCOUNTABLE NOUN
Tolerance is the quality of allowing other people to say what they want and believe what they want, even if you do not agree with them.

torture TRANSITIVE VERB
To **torture** someone means to deliberately cause them great pain in order to punish them or make them reveal information.

traitor COUNTABLE NOUN
A **traitor** is someone who betrays their country by helping or supporting their enemies.

tsar COUNTABLE NOUN, TITLE NOUN
In Russia, **tsar** was the name used for their emperor until the Revolution in 1917.

tumour COUNTABLE NOUN
A **tumour** is a mass of diseased or abnormal cells that has grown in someone's body, and that can cause cancer.

upper-middle class ADJECTIVE
Upper-middle class people and families belong at the top level of the middle classes, but are not upper class or noble.

vicar COUNTABLE NOUN
A **vicar** is a priest in the Church of England, usually one who is responsible for a particular church and the people who live in that area.

will COUNTABLE NOUN
Someone's **will** is a legal document in which they say what should happen to their money and property after they die.

working class COUNTABLE NOUN
The working class or **working classes** are the people in a society who do not own much property, who have low social status, and whose work involves physical skills rather than intellectual skills.
ADJECTIVE
Working-class people or families belong to the working classes.

Collins
English Readers

AMAZING PEOPLE READERS AT OTHER LEVELS:

Level 1

Amazing Inventors
978-0-00-754494-3

Amazing Women
978-0-00-754493-6

Amazing Leaders
978-0-00-754492-9

Amazing Performers
978-0-00-754508-7

**Amazing Entrepreneurs and
Business People**
978-0-00-754501-8

Level 2

Amazing Aviators
978-0-00-754495-0

Amazing Mathematicians
978-0-00-754503-2

Amazing Architects and Artists
978-0-00-754496-7

Amazing Medical People
978-0-00-754509-4

Amazing Composers
978-0-00-754502-5

Level 3

Amazing Explorers
978-0-00-754497-4

Amazing Performers
978-0-00-754505-6

Amazing Writers
978-0-00-754498-1

Amazing Scientists
978-0-00-754510-0

Amazing Philanthropists
978-0-00-754504-9

Visit **www.collinselt.com/readers** for language activities, teacher's
notes, and to find out more about the series.

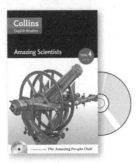